Organic Gardening

Beginner Guide on Starting an Organic Garden

copyrighted@2022

Brian Batchelor

Table of Contents

Chapter One 2

   How to Start an Organic Garden 2

Chapter Two 24

   Ways of Breaking Ground 24

Chapter Three 49

   Organic 49

Chapter Four 71

   Garden Maintenance 71

Chapter One

How to Start an Organic Garden

Are you thinking of starting a garden, but doing it the old-fashioned way without pesticides? Organic Gardening can be a lot of fun, but there are some steps you will need to take before you start.

I headed to my organic garden on a cool summer night, cut emerald zucchini from a piece of squash, pulled a handful of sugary snap from the grapes, sliced rosemary and thyme from the vegetable gardens, and pulled out kale to get some tasty Italian homemade meal.

In a world of uncertainty, climate change, and food insecurity, gardening remains important. There is something special about growing humble seeds into fruit meal directly from the Earth. It is a reconnection of our core roots.

Whether you want to be independent, connect with nature, or just enjoy high quality food, starting an organic garden can be the most rewarding activity you have ever done. If you have a "green thumb" or a "black thumb", it does not matter. Nature is known for being forgiving and gardens are places for exploration and recreation.

Garden Basics

Most people these days make organic gardens very difficult. We have forgotten that our ancestors found a way to grow food beyond their eyes to look at nature and their hands to feel the earth. There is plenty of time to learn, develop, and perfect your gardening skills.

Unfortunately, you will not be able to plant a complete organic garden with just a few tips. This guide, however, aims to give you all the information you need to successfully start your organic garden, even if you have never picked up a garden shovel before. Let's get into the basics.

What is Organic Gardening?

Using only natural methods and essentials means that your garden is organic.

You probably want to start a garden to live a healthy and organic life, so the use of toxic chemicals is not on the table.

Gardening is about growing plants in accordance with Nature. The environment does not use man-made harmful chemicals to kill insects or weeds, and it does not disturb the soil or plant monocultures as do industrial farms do.

Organic gardening takes an ecological approach to growing food. Most importantly, organic eating ensures that you feed your family as healthy food as possible and maintain a healthy environment in your yard and garden for years to come.

Organic Gardening Rules

There are several rules to follow in an organic garden.

The term "organic" is technically regulated by the USDA and refers to a whole set of developing practices, including:

- No synthetic fertilizer

- zero synthetic pesticides, fungicides or herbicides

- No GMOs

- Enhancing the science of soil biology

- Growing a variety of crops

- Use of compost or other organic matter

- Buy only organic, untreated seeds

- Planting pollinator habitat

Since you are not a production farm, you do not have to worry about all the nuances of organic certification, but you can still benefit by looking at labels such as Organic certified seed or OMRI (Organic Material Review

Institute) for certified soil, fertilizers, and amendments.

Most Important Tools

There are many tools to choose from, but keeping them simple will go a long way.

There are many different tools that are important for every gardener to have. Each of these tools has a different purpose, and will not be wasted as you begin to build your first organic garden.

- Wheelbarrow
- Shovel
- Rake
- Wide fork
- Planting Knife (Hori Hori)
- Measurement tape
- Pipe or watering can

Designing Your Garden

Starting an organic garden can be very fun, but it is important that you do not go without a plan! An organic garden is an venture for years to come, so you want to make sure your hard work is not in vain. It also helps to understand the basics of organic gardening so that you can really enjoy yourself and the fruits of your labor. Here's how to put one together for success.

Growing Area

Knowing your hardiness area will help you take the first steps to your organic garden.

First things first, look at your weather. What are the coldest and hottest temperatures? This will determine how "certain" certain plants are in your area.

Crop hardiness simply refers to how a plant withstands cold. For example, garlic can survive in deep colds, broccoli tolerates soft frost, and tomatoes often die in the first frost (unless protected).

You can easily get "lost in the weeds" with climate information. It is best to start easily by deciding on your growing area and using it to plan your garden.

Use the USDA Hardiness Zone map, simply enter your zip code and use the colored key to determine your location. If you are on the edge of a growing area (e.g. between 5a and 5b), use the colder to be safe (5a). When you start buying plants and seeds, many labels will include a hardiness zone.

Microclimates

Rooftop gardens will have a different microclimate than a park or yard, even if they are on the same block!

The microclimate is a small, well-ventilated area with different climates from the surrounding climate. Manhattan's city concrete floor will be much hotter and drier than the grassy plains of Central Park. Similarly, different areas of your yard will have different temperatures, sunlight levels, soil types, and drainage.

Where to Place Your Garden

You will need to ask yourself a number of questions to determine exactly where your organic garden should go.

To find the best place to put your garden, start by looking at the microclimates in your yard. Ask yourself:

• Where is there full sunlight during the day?

• Do the trees provide shade in certain areas of the day / season?

• Are there steep slopes?

• Are there areas where the grass seems to thrive compared to areas where there is less growth?

• What is the most practical and accessible location for your garden?

• Is there a nearby forest or wild place where animals can wait to eat your lettuce?

• How much does the temperature change in this area of your yard?

• Which area is closest to the water source (spigot or pipe)?

Ideally, your garden should be as flat as possible, have good drainage (not including rainwater), high sunlight (or just a little shade), and be close to a house or tool shed for easy access.

Choosing Your Garden Beds

A bed is a place where vegetables, herbs, or perennials are grown. It is helpful to separate garden beds in other areas of the yard so that grass does not penetrate. Clear beds also help keep children and pets out of the garden.

In terms of shape, curvy artsy garden beds are very fun, but can be difficult to maintain and water. That is why gardeners grow in straight lines. However, if you choose a wild or traditional garden, somehow, create crazy beds!

Raised Beds

Many organic gardens are located in raised garden beds, as they are easy to maintain.

Raised beds are the best option for small urban and suburban gardeners. They do not require complex construction skills and work well on existing lawns or poor soil because they build on top. It is also easy to care for the grass or wood chip around the raised beds. Also, if you have a gopher or rodent problem, it is easy to put a piece of hardware cloth under the raised bed to prevent them from digging under your vegetables.

Suggested beds are big planting boxes that can be made to fit your style and budget. Commonly used raw materials (double check that they are not pressure-treated or painted), large logs, or paved beef cattle. For the elderly or those with back pain, you can design raised beds 2-3 meters long to bend slightly, but remember that this will require a lot of soil or compost to fill the boxes themselves.

In-Ground

Many organic gardeners prefer to plant directly in the soil.

In-ground beds are like a production farm or market garden. These are best if you have extra space, a tight budget, and / or a healthy soil that has not been treated with herbicides. The best way to start in-ground beds is to use the tarping method described below.

Next, use tape measure, rope, and stakes to mark your beds (usually we set our beds 30 "wide and 10-50 feet tall). Make sure you leave a path between each bed that gives you enough space to stand, bend, tow a wheelbarrow, and set up a harvest bag.

If your beds are marked, we recommend that you add a layer of compost over each bed so that it rises above the ground. You also can use the lasagna method. If your soil is already in good condition, you can just broadfork, rake, and get ready to plant!

Perennial Landscaping beds

Many gardeners prefer attractive landscapes to complement the beauty of their yard or home.

You may be familiar with the typical landscape beds around your home. This garden bed style is suitable for perennials, which are woody plants and plants that live year after year. The opposite is true for annual plants, which must be replanted every year from the beginning or seed. Lots of vegetables for the year. Fruit trees, low berries, many herbs, and ornamental plants of the earth usually last longer.

To create landscape beds, first apply tarping or mulching existing vegetation. Mulch can be compost, topsoil, planks, or other weed control material. Next, make your beds with bricks or stones. You will need to measure the recommended space between perennials and consider how large they will be in full size. Double digging of planting holes for perennials such as certain berries or apple trees will help them to emerge and bear fruit faster.

Chapter Two
Ways of Breaking Ground

There are many different ways to successfully breaking ground in your garden. Some are more involved than others, and those who take less effort, can often end up producing better yields, so keep that in mind. Let's take a look at some of the most common ways to break the ground.

Lazy Way: Tarping

Plastic tarps can be helpful when starting an organic garden.

It may surprise you, but simple tarps are a great companion of the gardener. You can use tarp (heavy with stones or sandbags) to set up new garden areas with minimal effort. Just measure and place the tarp on the existing grass or soil. It will eliminate weeds and grass in 2-3 weeks, depending on the weather and plants. It can be left for a long time to get better results.

Look under the tarp to see if the grass is completely dead. After that, you can start building your own raised wooden beds or layering organic matter as lasagna-style in-ground beds under the lasagna style described below. I recommend covering your paths with wooden planks, leaves, or straw to keep the grass from growing.

The Fast Way: Mow + Mulch

One of the quickest ways to start a garden is to mow back the grass and add mulch.

If you are looking to have a garden at the end of the day, your best bet is to use a lawn mower to cut the existing vegetation as low as possible. Next, choose a grass cover. This could be cardboard (no tape), newspaper, leaves, or grass (not hay). This can also be done under your planting boxes when building raised beds.

Lastly, cover with a 3-6" layer of compost or topsoil (make sure it has not been treated with chemicals). It's like a quick garden! After some sweat and wheelbarrow trowing, you will be ready to plant.

For the Best Soil: Lasagna Style

This gardening style is best for the soil as the material decomposes, providing rich nutrients to your soil and crops!

Hugelkultur or "lasagna gardening" has been used in

Germany for centuries to create growing soil from the ground up. If you are starting a garden in a very compact area, an open area with weeds, or grass, lasagna-style gardening will help you get started right away and build fertile soil for many years to come.

The layering of organic matter is what sets the "lasagna" in the lasagna garden.

Organic matter is simply dead or decaying plant or animal matter, including:

- Compost

- Old Manure

- Grass

- Leaves

- Pieces of grass

- Branches and sticks

Use these materials to build a lasagna bed of blooming soil that will break down over time. The materials that will take the longest to be broken down (branches, sticks, wood) go down, and the upper layers will move on to more fragile items (grass, leaves, clippings of grass, old manure). The top should be 3-5 inches of high quality compost or topsoil.

Not Recommended: Rototilling

I do not recommend rototilling for a number of reasons.

Another note about the establishment of garden beds: it is better to avoid rototilling. A rototiller or tiller is a machine that grinds the ground using metal tools. This may seem like a good way to start a garden at first, but it destroys the soil structure very quickly and eventually causes concrete-like congestion (especially in clay soils).

Congestion creates anaerobic (non-oxygen) conditions that allow organic matter to grow in plants and make it difficult for plant roots to reach the ground. Rototillers also undermine important soil biology that helps keep gardens healthy and thriving.

Lastly, tilling will make weed issues worse by spreading perennial weeds and annual weed seeds. It is best to use the above methods of no or till method to make your garden start at the right foot.

Planning Your Garden

Building a garden is a time full of joy and happiness. But before you start throwing seeds and planting them in your new beds, it helps to plan what you want to grow and the needs of each type of plant.

What Vegetables Do You Like to Eat?

Knowing that you will enjoy the final product helps motivate you when things get dirty!

The biggest mistake gardeners make is to grow many plants that they do not enjoy eating.

Exploration is important, but you also want to enjoy the fruits of your labor!

If you don't like radishes, don't just grow them. Or at least try a special kind like the Purple Daikons or the colorful Rainbow Radishes, rather than the old boring red radish at the grocery store.

When talking about grocery stores, keep in mind that vegetables from your garden will probably have more flavor than the supermarket. That said, some vegetables (like potatoes) are inexpensive to buy, so you should only grow them if you have a very special variety you want to try (like Huckleberry Golds- yum!)

An open mind is important for any gardener, but make sure you plant food that will make it accessible to the dinner table! Make a list of the top 10 vegetables you want to put first in your garden.

Levels of Difficulty in vegetable planting

There are many different vegetables to choose from. Some will be more difficult than others. This means you will want to make sure you have the right expectations or some additional guidelines in case you have problems and need to resolve the problem. Let's take a look at several common plants and their weight levels.

Easy to grow

Sweet Corn

Radishes

Turnips

Kale

Spinach

Lettuce

Moderately difficult

Cucumbers

Tomatoes

Cantaloupe

Pepper

Strawberries

Eggplant

Very advanced

Carrots

Broccoli

Cauliflower

Cabbage

Fruit Trees

Vine & Bush Berries

Crop Planning

You would not travel on a road trip without a map, would you? Well, do not start a garden without a plan. This is your seasonal guide to expand your space and grow plenty of healthy food!

Start by looking at your list of the most important vegetables you have ever made before. Label each crop as "Cool Season" or "Warm Season" based on the following chart:

Cool Season Crops

Summer Season Crops

Snow Days

Do some research to find out when frost is expected so you can better plan for it.

You can find the best planting dates for your garden based on weather history data. Go back to your USDA growing area number and use it to view your region's estimated first and last frost days on the Old Gardener's Almanac website.

The last day of the snow is the measure of the "safe zone" to plant frost-tender plants in the spring. The first snow date is the estimated first freeze in the fall or winter. Summer plants need to be planted inside this window. Row cloth or row cover (such as Agribon or Remay) can extend these days by providing an extra layer of sun protection.

Plant Spacing

The most common mistake for beginners is to space things up very closely. Like humans, plants get stressed when they are crowded together. Cramming things can result in less yields. Give everyone their own space while you still benefit the most from your garden area.

Think of your garden as a grid (some people like to use string in beds to mark the grid). You should consider the space between each plant, and the space between each row.

Choose Seeds or Starts

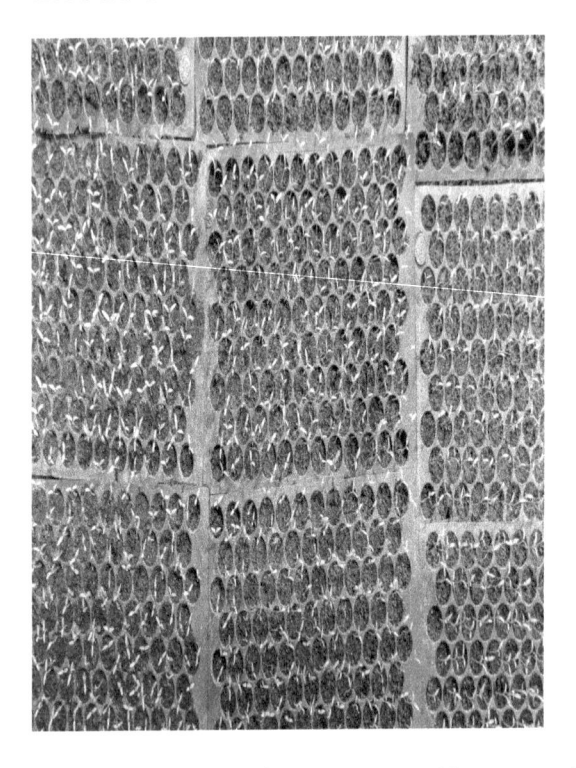

Getting started can save time and ensure a healthy plant.

The onset of seed is a perfect connection to an organic food source. However, the beginning of the crop is easy and accessible to novice gardeners. When you start your first garden, you may want to buy baby plants from a nursery, tropical plant, or a nearby organic farm. This will save you trouble setting up seed launches, trays, and / or small nursery.

Benefits of Buying Plant starts

• Strong healthy plants that is ready to be laid down

• No initial seed setup required

• Best in cold climates because the plants have a beginning in a professional greenhouse

• "Quick" garden results

• Easy for beginners and kids

Disadvantages of buying Plant Starts

• It is more expensive than starting from seed

- Limited types available in nurseries

- They can have roots or overgrow their pots (avoid buying first in late spring)

- Need to source organic plants (Home Depot and Lowes implants are usually chemically treated)

Direct seeding vs. Transplanting

Direct seeding means sowing the seeds directly in the garden, rather than starting with the trays first. This is much more straightforward than indoor seed germination and does not require initial seed setup.

However, you need a watering system or you will be hand-watering with a pipe every day. Seeds should remain wet until germination. They may also need protection from rodents or adverse weather conditions. Plants with straight seeds often need to be pruned to have the right space.

Transplanting is the act of planting a baby plant that starts (from pots or trays) to the garden. These plants have a beginning and are already established. They are especially good in colder climates with more growing seasons because you can get your garden moving faster in the spring. You can also re-install the start in the exact space they need, so no reduction is required.

Which Vegetables Prefer Direct Seeding?

These plants will not survive re-planting or do not really like root disturbance. It is best to plant them directly in the garden and water them well until germination.

• Beans

• Beets (can be replanted, but directly sown)

• Carrots

• Maize (can be planted in a cold climate, but planted directly)

• Parsnips

• Radishes

• Sugar Snap Peas

• Turnips

• Cucurbits (cantaloupe, melons, cucumbers, squash, pumpkins, etc. can be replanted, but usually do best when planted directly)

Types of Seeds

The seed world can be slightly confusing, so it is important to understand the differences between each item. When buying seeds, it is best to get a seed catalog in the winter so that you can learn the variety and use all the educational information provided by different seed companies.

Chapter Three

Organic

One of the best seed varieties for your organic garden is organic seeds.

Certified organic seeds were grown in ways controlled by the

USDA National Organic Program. They have not been treated with pesticides, fungicides, herbicides, or synthetic fertilizers. They are also guaranteed to be non-GMO, as genetically modified seeds are strictly restricted to living organisms. You will find a green or black mark of the USDA Certified Organic seal on these types of seed packs.

It is important to note that many species are not organically occurring (for a variety of reasons). Even on certified biological farms, some seeds have to be acquired normally due to their lack. As long as the seeds have not been treated with fungicides or fertilizers, they are still safe for use in organic production. Search for "untreated" or "NOP-compliant" pellets.

Open Pollinated

These seeds need pollinators, such as bees or wind, to pollinate and bear fruit.

If the seed is open pollinated (OP), it means that it can breed freely with its neighbors. If pollinated by other plants of the same type, it will produce real offspring. OP seeds are not hybridized, so it is the best way for anyone interested in seed storage. OP seeds also need wind, pollinator, or people to move their flowers to bear fruit.

The only warning here is that, if you grow many varieties of OP squash, for example, a bee can easily disperse pollen and produce unique seeds that are not really true in the original varieties.

Heirloom

Tomatoes are a popular heirloom seed option.

Heirlooms are old lineages of plant species, often described as being passed down from generation to generation for at least 50 years. Similar to the family legacy, these types of vegetables are similar to the old ones. Their genes have been preserved from the past. Heirloom tomatoes like 'Brandywine' and 'Cherokee Purple' are among the most popular heirloom seeds. All heirlooms are open pollinated or self-pollinated, so they are also suitable for seed saving.

Hybrid

Taking the best qualities of two varieties of the same plant creates a mixture of that plant.

Hybrid seeds are made by crossing two different varieties of the same plant. For example, a vegetable grower may want the firmness and taste of one type of cucumber cross-resistant to another type of cucumber. Over the years, cross-pollinating and selective breeding, F1 hybrid seeds are created and their rows are maintained by seed companies. There are many varieties of Certified Organic F1 hybrid seeds available.

Although not a complete match, hybrid seeds can be compared to breeding specialized dogs such as Goldendoodles. The dog breeder selects the best female Golden Retriever and the best male Poodle, mixes them together, and creates puppies with different characteristics. Puppies of those original parents will not always produce genes like the original cross. To keep the genealogy, only certain dogs will be reborn.

Like Goldendoodle puppies, hybrid seeds do not preserve the original variety, so they are not good options for gardeners who want to save seeds. Descendants will be very different and have many different traits for first parents.

GMO

Organic gardens should not contain GMO, or Genetically Modified Organisms, seeds.

Seeds of Genetically Modified Organisms (GMOs) are often the most controversial in the agricultural world. They are banned from the production of organic but widely used in conventional chemical gardening. GMO seeds contain genes that are used in the laboratory environment to produce certain traits. For example, resistance to RoundUp spraying, or bacterial poisoning called Bt that kills caterpillars.

Happily, GMOs are common in the agricultural sector such as soybeans, wheat, alfalfa, corn, and potatoes. Gardeners generally do not have to worry about GMO seeds and will not benefit from using them. All Organic certified seeds are not GMO.

Planting Your Organic Garden

Once you have built your garden beds, planned your planting dates, and found your seed or starting plant, it is time to dig! Planting is a very fun part of gardening (besides harvesting anyway), so you will want to choose a happy sunny day and prepare your tools early.

Useful Planting Tools

It helps to have simple gardening tools on hand before you start.

- Hori Hori (planting knife)
- Measurement tape
- A small cup or seed bowl
- Hand seeder for very small seeds
- Pipe or watering can

How to Start a Seed

Planting seeds in trays at the beginning of the season can give you a quick start to your garden.

In early spring, many gardeners like to start the season with seed starters. The main goal is to have seedlings ready for planting as soon as the weather allows. Some of the easiest seeds to start at home include tomatoes, basil, marigolds, nasturtium, cosmos, lettuce, kale, broccoli, chard, and bok choy.

To put things in perspective, check your seed packets and look for phrases like "start seed indoors four to six weeks before the final frost." Count back on your calendar and make sure you plant inside that window.

Simplest setup includes:

• Seed starting trays

• Bottom trays (to catch the water)

• A high quality potting mix

• Large south-facing window.

• Additional Lighting: If you do not have enough organic light, your seeds will become "leggy" as they reach the window. This is where you can bring in extra light, such as fluorescent strip lamps hanging over the starting point of the seed.

To start seeding:

1. Fill your trays with potting mix (don't mix them too much, a simple pat will do)

2. Make small indents in the cell of each tray, like a small hole for your seeds to rest

3. Plant your seeds to a depth of about twice the size of the seed

4. Cover them with a light layer of soil

5. Keep moist, but do not get wet

6. Hardening-off: Once the seedling has grown to 2-5"in height and the roots are full of cells, prepare to transplant by gradually moving them outside. For example, you can cover them with a row cover on the balcony a few nights before planting. This process allows the weaker plants to adapt to the outside temperature of the night before they reach the garden.

How to Direct Sow

Another option is to plant the seeds directly in the ground when the weather is good.

As mentioned above, certain plants are best planted directly in the garden.

1. Prepare your beds with a thin 1-2 ounces [1-2 ounces] of compost or topsoil.

2. Rake well and smooth.

3. Use a rake handle to draw a shallow line in the soil.

4. Carefully pour your seed pack into a deep bowl or cup.

5. Drop your seeds in a recommended spacing (or slightly dense - you can stay thin later).

6. Cover with a light layer of soil, making sure that the seeds do not rise above the level of the soil when irrigated. But also make sure that it does not overheat or that it will have difficulty reaching the light.

7. Water well and retain moisture, but do not get wet, until it sprouts.

8. Use small scissors or needle-tip pruners to thin as you want.

How to Plant

You can start your own seed or buy them in a nursery, and plant them in your garden.

Transplanting is an easy and child-friendly way to plant your garden. Your seedlings should be healthy, green, and already strong (adapt to the outside temperature).

1. Prepare garden beds by weeding and raking clean.

2. Slowly loosen the seedling starts from their cells by pressing down on the tray until they release the root system (be careful not to disturb the roots).

3. Use the Hori Hori planting knife to create a hole as deep as the root ball. Many plants have to be transplanted to the same soil level as the ones in their cell packs. Very different tomatoes, which can be planted deep and will take root throughout the stem.

4. Use your tape measure to space all other plants (they will look far apart, but don't worry- they will fill the space as they grow!).

5. Properly "water" the new transplant to help them adapt to their new soil.

6. If you prefer, cover with a row cover (covered with bricks, sandbags, or local foundation) until your plants are established.

Chapter Four

Garden Maintenance

Caring for the garden is a refreshing and inspiring activity if you stay on top of garden maintenance. However, if you allow things to get out of hand you may begin to dread the prospect of going out and inspecting your plants. Gardening should not be a difficult task, but it does require careful attention and problem solving.

The secret to a happy garden (and a happy gardener) is simply setting aside 10-15 minutes daily or more to explore the garden, pull weeds, inspect watering, inspect insects, and harvest ripe vegetables. For more hot summer days, you can choose to explore your garden more often. And on a perfect 70 degree sunny mornings, you may find yourself sitting quietly with the plants enjoying the fruits of your labor.

Watering and Irrigation

Any garden should have access to water, whether it is irrigation system or hose.

Small gardens do not require complex irrigation systems, but you do need regular access to water. Keep a hose and spray nozzle close at all times, especially when seeds are germinating. You can also set drip irrigation or soaker hoses on timers to save water and effort. Over-irrigation (i.e. spraying) is generally not recommended because it covers a large area and promotes more weeds.

Controlling Pests organically

Unfortunately, we are not the only ones who want to eat hot lettuce or delicious garden carrots. There will definitely be insects. Part of the gardening is combing with fists and working with nature rather than opposing it. There is no need to immerse your garden in pesticides to eradicate all pests and damage your family or your local ecosystem. Happily, there are many strategies for controlling pests in a garden.

Introduction to Biocontrol

Ladybugs are an example of biological control as they feed on harmful aphids.

Biological control, or biocontrol, is the act of controlling insects using organic enemies and predators. A few popular biocontrol agents include ladybugs, parasitic wasps, and spiders. These predatory insects feed on insects and eagerly reproduce when numerous insects are found.

Like a cat that controls rats in the yard (another type of biocontrol), insect predators keep insects at a manageable level. You do not want to kill all the insects with a wide range of pesticides, because the insects will come back faster than the predators.

It is the same if you kill all the mountain lions in the area; the rabbits will soon be full!

Ecological balance is the main source of biocontrol in the organic garden. The goal is not to eliminate all insects; otherwise they will not be eaten by predators and will migrate.

Biological control can be active (classical biological control) or passive (conservation biological control). Classical biological control means purchasing and releasing predator-like ladybugs to combat existing pest infestations. Passive conservation biocontrol is very protective. It involves creating a habitat for beneficial insects to stay in your garden and create an organic balance.

Planting a Beneficial Insect Habitat

Cosmos flowers attract predators, so planting some nearby will give your garden an advantage.

Some plants make them pick up the exact type of insects we want in the garden: ladybugs, spiders, beetles, caterpillars, lacewings, hoverflies, prayer mantis, and insect wasps (don't worry, these wasps target insects like worms).

It is best to plant an insect habitat near your garden beds as much as possible. Use them as a touch of a beautiful garden setting, or just "blend" the beneficial type that blooms in front of all the beds.

I spread white alyssum and calendula around all my plants to impress with the added beauty and "complementary planting" approach. A nice bonus is that these plants also attract and nourish local insects. Besides, who does not love beautiful flowers?

Here are a few amazing plants to attract (and retain) other predators in your garden:

- White alyssum
- Phacelia
- Dill
- Yarrow
- Angelica
- Cosmos
- Coriander (flowering cilantro)
- Queen Anee's Lace
- Fenel
- Prairie Sunflower
- Dandelion
- Hairy vetch
- Tansy
- Lavender globe lily

Using the Row Cover

One solution that is effective in controlling organic pest is to use a row cover.

Exclusion is another easy way to control organic pests. Basically, you simply cover off the bugs in your plants with a lucent cloth called a row cover. Row cover is best used on brassicas ("Cole crops" such as kale, seedling, turnip, bok chok, cabbage, cauliflower, etc.) to prevent flea beetles from infesting the leaves. The cover of the line also prevents cabbage moths from laying larvae.

You can also use row cover to provide extra warmth to newly planted seedlings or plants with warmer climates such as watermelons. In the spring, I use a thick layer cover for most of my pre-installed inserts to give them extra protection.

There are many layers of row cover that offer different levels of embellishment, so make sure you get a very light row cover in the hottest seasons of the year (which are often when insects like beetles are most common). You do not want to put your plants under the cloth.

Insect Barrier Netting

Similar to the row cover, ProtekNet is a special lucent netting material to prevent bugs, while allowing water and sunlight to shine. These are best in very hot climates (where the row cover is very hot) and problems with very small insects such as thrips. Wire hoops are recommended for best results.

All Organic Insecticides

Using natural or organic ingredients in the spray can effectively eliminate pests.

I suggest you make your own safe and organic sprays to deal with pest problems. I never buy insect repellent, even organic approved products. Very safe and cheap to make your own! Here are a few DIY tricks for common insects.

Biodegradable Soap and Cayenne Pepper: spicy peppers are a great way to kill mites and thrips, as well as repel flies. Add a few drops of biodegradable soap and 2 tablespoons of cayenne pepper to one liter of water and let stand overnight. Apply a spray bottle directly on the leaves of the affected plant.

Tomato Leaf Spray:
Nightshades (tomatoes, peppers, and the potato family) are toxic to many insects such as aphids and worms due to the alkaloids in the leaves. Soak tomato leaves in water and put them in mister bottle for use.

Insecticide Soap: Biodegradable soap is sudsy and melts the outer layer of pests such as mites, aphids, scales, and thrips. Simply mix a teaspoon with a gallon of water and spray the plants directly in the morning or evening (not in direct sunlight).

Horsetail Fungal Spray: Equisetum is an olden plant usually called horsetail. It grows in swampy areas and is surprisingly anti-fungal. Simply collect the horsetail needles and dip them in hot water as a tea. Let the tea cool down and apply it directly to plants with fever or other fungal infections. This will also strengthen the leaf cells to prevent future problems.

Slug Beer Trap: Slugs, for any reason, are engrossed with bee. If you have a slug problem, fill a shallow plastic container with cheap beer, place it on the ground at a low level, and watch the slugs fall and drown in their happy hour.

Dealing with Weeds

It is best to get in front of the weed before it becomes a problem.

Weeds are a nuisance to the presence of any gardener! They compete with our plants for land, water, sunlight, and nutrients. Plus, they just don't look good. When choosing a weed garden, prevention is important. They get younger and younger before they cause serious problems.

Weed Control Strategies

• No-Till: When the soil is plowed, it grinds the roots of perennial weeds and disperses annual weed seeds. Rototilling creates more problems than it should. Cultivation also disrupts the soil environment and promotes more rapid bacterial-dominant weeds.

- Never Let the Weeds Go to Seed! Don't just do it! Get them early.

- Tarping: As with establishing a garden, sometimes tarp is the best way to remove weeds in the middle of the season and get a fresh start.

- Hoeing: A great option for standing up and weeding. Try a stirrup hoe or wire hoe for best results.

- Hand Crafting: Just pluck them out and get them out of the garden!

Disease Prevention

A healthy soil is the best way to fight disease, but sometimes organic spray is needed to treat a plant-borne disease.

The first and best way to prevent common plant diseases is to create healthy soil! The soil is similar to the external immune system and the digestive system of the plant. If you have used the lasagna garden method or the compost-heavy method above, you are probably on your way to building a healthy soil ecosystem. As humans, unhealthy or weak plants are at greater risk of disease. If you keep them happy and healthy from the start, diseases will not be a problem.

However, wind problems such as powdery mildew or blight may arise. The dots or marks on the leaves of the plant should never be scary, but you should be careful how you can prevent these problems.

Strategies for Preventing Plant Diseases

• Use appropriate spacing to ensure air flow between plants

- Maintain a healthy soil using compost and non-tillage methods

- Cut and remove diseased leaves

- Avoid over-watering (spraying)

- Use the horsetail herb tea spray described above to strengthen plant cell walls

- Avoid excessive watering

- Plant-resistant species. This is the most important method of prevention. Certain types of seeds are raised to withstand serious diseases. Learn about the varieties in your seed catalog and choose the most resistant ones!

Organic Amendments

In some plants, coffee processing can act as an organic fertilizer.

Organic fertilizers are easy to find in large garden stores today. There is no need for r other synthetics because these types of nitrogen actually damage the microbes in the soil and give your plants a "quick fix" rather than providing a little bit of organic nutrients.

For amendments and fertilizers, always check the label "OMRI approved for organic production". Always make sure you use only the recommended amount (weigh carefully). Fertilizer burns can still occur with organic fertilizers and can cause more damage than good for your garden.

Organic Fertilizers

- Liquid fish or hydrolysate fish
- Feather feeds
- Fish meal
- Blood food
- Composted manure
- casting of worms

- Rock dust

- Azomite

- Pelleted chicken manure

Season End Tips

Preparing your garden beds for the winter is a great way to make sure they are in the right condition for the spring.

At the end of the growing season, you can finally relax and enjoy your varied harvests. I hope you have saved some cucumbers dipped in salt water, dried tomatoes, frozen pesto, and other signs of summer abundance. To increase your yield next season, it is important to prepare the beds for the winter.

Remove Plant Material

Instead of letting the plants sit and rot all winter, it is better to cut them at the base (leaving the roots firm) and compost the material. This helps prevent diseases and keeps hungry winter animals away. Some plants, such as kale, garlic, and cabbage, can be left in the garden all winter to harvest continuously (depending on your climate).

Annual Additions of Compost

At the end or beginning of each season, I would add a small amount of compost to all my garden beds to keep the soil happy and well nurtured. It is important to get high quality compost or learn to make your own. Worm compost (vermicast) or professionally fertilized compost are good options to replenish nutrients and help build soil structure.

Putting Your Garden to Bed

To put your gardens "to sleep" at the end of the season, I highly recommend covering the soil to protect it from winter rain or snow. The best mulch is fallen maple leaves. You can also use unprocessed dry grass, tarp, or cover crop such as peas and oats.

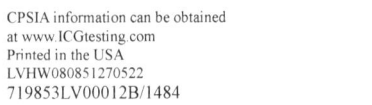

CPSIA information can be obtained
at www.ICGtesting.com
Printed in the USA
LVHW080851270522
719853LV00012B/1484